CHOICE OF A MARRIAGE PARTNER?

LOOK BEFORE YOU LEAP!

SOLOMON B. LAWRENCE

The reader should consult pastors and Christian relationship counsellors in all matters relating to their choice of a marriage partner. Neither the author nor the publisher can be held responsible for errors or any consequences of using the information contained here.

DEDICATION

This eBook is dedicated to The Trinity-In-Council: God The Father, God The Son, and God The Holy Spirit, for saving my soul and inspiring me to write this transformational eBook for the emancipation of every Christian single worldwide as it relates to doing the will of God in marriage, and being Biblically guided in choosing the right marriage partner.

I'm also dedicating this eBook to my darling wife, Olayinka, a daughter of Zion, for her love and prayers in the course of our seventeen years of marriage and to my two god-fearing sons, Oluwaferanmi (The Diplomat) and Oluwadarasimi (The Prof) for responding well to godly wisdom on parenting.

Finally, I acknowledge all the Pastors whose teaching moulded me and enhanced my knowledge of my Lord and Saviour, Jesus Christ. Time and space would not permit me to mention all of them. Pastor E A Adeboye (The General Overseer of The Redeemed Christian Church of God, Worldwide) and Bishop David Oyedepo (The Presiding Bishop of The Living Faith Church, Worldwide) are keys to the success of this Book! Thank you, sirs.

INTRODUCTION

As ordained by God Almighty, marriage is meant to be enjoyed and not endured. A happy marriage is based on God's blueprint or formula through His Word. Anything short of this will spell disaster.

Therefore, this e-book is written to help and guide God-fearing men and women contemplating marriage!

For a marriage to be solid, fulfilling, and successful, God has to be involved first and foremost in the individual's life, leading to making sound decisions on whom to choose as a marriage partner.

The question of whom to marry has to be looked at from the Christian perspective based upon the unchanging and infallible Word of God; this is vital if the Christian single must enjoy marital bliss.

Hence, this Book has highlighted sixteen (16) things a Christian single must consider before marriage. It is my earnest prayer that you will find this helpful. I pray that as you read and take steps accordingly, the Holy Spirit will grant you understanding and help you choose the right marriage partner with peace of mind in Jesus' name.

THE WORD OF GOD

"When you allow God's Word to determine your actions, you will never miss his intervention in your situation." - Bishop George Amos.

Dear single brother or sister, for you to realize your dream of marrying in the God-given way, His Word in your life must be a dominant factor. Not tradition or what people say but what the Word of God says. Why?

Let us take a look at what God says in His Word:

"Flowers and grass fade away, but what our God has said will never change." - Is. 40:8 (CEV).

You have to choose whether you want to add to the plethora of problems the society is grappling with regarding divorce vis-à-vis failed marriages, or you want to be exempted from such by enjoying your marriage till the Lord Jesus Christ returns.

Once again, the value you place on the Word of God will reflect in your decision-making when choosing a marriage partner. God's desire for all His children, including you, is to achieve experience and swim in the ocean of success in all areas of your life, marriage inclusive.

God said in His Word:

"This Book of the Law shall not depart from your mouth, but you shall meditate in it day and night, that you may observe to do according to all that is written in it. For then you will make your way prosperous, and then you will have good success." - Joshua 1:8 (NKJV).

Undeniably, there are novels, magazines, biographies, and other secular books with lots of marriage advice. Yet, only the Bible–God's written Book–can guarantee sound advice that leads to a lifetime of marital bliss.

The world is changing. Fashion is changing. Surprisingly, the world's view about marriage continues to change. The Bible refers to these as "flowers" and "grass." They ultimately fade away with time, but God's Word never changes. It is very reliable.

Many women, including some single Christian sisters, wear crazy clothes that expose all their sensitive parts in the name of moving with the current fashion trend. Even if others are doing it, must you, a child of God, be a culprit? (Prov. 1:10).

Those who succumb to these changes reap terrible consequences. But those who submit to the influence of God's holy spirit reap great results. The Word of God may be "old," but it is relevant in every generation (Heb 13:8).

As an aspiring husband or wife, you must align your choices and decisions with God's Word. Otherwise, danger and regret will be the outcome. I am reminded of what the Word of God says in proverbs 14:12:

"There is a way that seems right to a man, but its end is the way of death."

Unfortunately, some of our Christian youth and singles are towing that path that seems right. The path that tradition, society, friends, and even family at times approve of is totally against God's Word.

I vividly remember when I went to my home town to intimate my people about my wedding. One of my elderly aunts called me aside to remind me of the general tradition or culture of putting your fiancé in the family way (i.e., ensure your wife gets pregnant first) before the wedding as an approved way of ensuring that she's fertile. I bluntly refused because that is contrary to what God says in His Word:

"Have respect for marriage...God will punish anyone who is immoral..." Heb 13:4 (CEV).

It is a gross lack of respect for marriage arrangements when a sister gets pregnant before her wedding day. Also, it is immoral for a sister and brother to indulge in sex before marriage. The Bible says God will punish such fellows. I need to ask you, what has culture or tradition done for us? Loads of problems in every sphere of life!

The Bible also urges every genuine child of God that: "if sinner entices you do not consent." Prov. 1:10 (KNJV).

Whether the sinner in question is your Father, Mother, Uncle, Aunt, or guardian, it does not matter. God says "do not consent" with their ungodly suggestions. Do not be pressurized! Do not be cajoled!! Do not be intimidated!!! God has great and big plans for your life.

How do I know? His Word says so!

"I will bless you with a future filled with hope – a future of success, not of suffering." Jer. 29:11 (CEV)

The New King James renders it this way.

"For I know the thoughts that I think towards you says the LORD, thoughts of peace and not of evil, to give you a future and a hope."

So what's the point? If you are a Christian single sister and a brother is pressuring you into having sex with him, do not consent! Even if he threatens to leave, do not consent! (Prov. 1:10)

Here is a Word for you:

Be happy and glad that God has exposed your current choice as not His plan for you.

However, if you are convinced that he is indeed for you, make him see reason with the Word of God, as we quoted earlier in Heb. 13:4. If the brother chooses not to listen, you had better run for your dear life and wait on God's leading and direction for a TRUE Child of God.

One of my mentors, a Pastor with RCCG (The Redeemed Christian Church of God), told me of an experience he once had while courting a sister. He thought or presumed that was God's choice for him until the sister began showing some amorous behaviour towards him contrary to what he had expected.

It happened that the sister paid the brother a visit in his two-room apartment, bringing with her some x-rated films for them to watch. She got access to the brother's apartment in his absence, and when he returned, he was shocked to see her watching such a sexually explicit film. He scolded her, but she saw nothing wrong with such movies. You can imagine that!

On another occasion, she requested the brother to kiss her lips before seeing her off. That was when my dear mentor called a spade a spade and ended the relationship. Listen to this: it is better to have a broken courtship than a broken marriage.

FOUNDATION

"If the foundations be destroyed, what can the righteous do?

Psalms 11:3

The question posed by the Word of God is a thought-provoking question! If you pause for a moment and meditate on the above scripture, you will discover that the righteous cannot do anything unless God divinely intervenes. But the damage or loss may take a lifetime to repair.

Before proceeding, let us isolate the word "Foundation" and define it. This is vital because planning for marriage is like building a house which starts with the type of marriage partner you choose. Much care must be taken in laying the foundation of such a marriage to stand the test of time.

What Is A Foundation?

Simply put, it means underlying principle. The underlying principle for a successful marriage starts with the brother or sister's devotion to the Word of God. For example, one of the underlying principles from the Word of God that helps a brother or sister make a good choice of a marriage partner is found in 2 Corinthians 6:14:

"Stay away from people who are not followers of the Lord. Can someone who is good get along with someone who is evil? Are light and darkness the same? - 2Cor. 6:14 (CEV)

As noted in the first chapter, the value a single brother or sister places on the Word of God will go a long way in who he or she chooses as a marriage partner.

The above scripture means a brother or sister MUST never choose to marry an unbeliever – someone not born-again. God has given us every instruction we need to succeed in every sphere of life if only we are willing and obedient.

Various Types Of Buildings

There are various types of buildings. There are face-me-I-face-you, bungalows, boy's quarters, duplexes, or mansions. The foundation of these houses differs. A three-storey building will require a deeper foundation with enough concretes, stones, and cement than a one-storey.

Hence, before you marry that brother or sister, please check out his/her foundation. The foundation has to be the SOLID ROCK type. And Jesus Christ is the Solid Rock!

Let us look at what His Word says about the foundation a single Christian brother or sister should watch out for when choosing a marriage partner:

"The foundation has already been built no person can build any other foundation. The foundation that has already been built is Jesus Christ." - 1Cor. 3:11 (Easy to read)

Does your prospective mate have the Lord Jesus Christ in them? Please be very careful! How then would you know if the fellow's foundation is of the Lord Jesus Christ?

Very simple. The Bible says, "by their fruits, you shall know them," and "out of the abundance of the heart, the mouth speaks."

Prayerfully monitor the fellow's behaviour and action, especially outside the church.

Many people coming to the church now parade themselves as devout Christians, and if carefree, you will be deceived. Some have been deceived already. Do not be one of them. Pay attention to the Word of God, which says:

"My dear friends, many false prophets are in the World now. So don't believe every spirit. But test the spirits to see if they are from God." - 1 Jn 4:1 (Easy to read)

That scripture alludes to the fact that many false Christians are in the church now. Hence be careful and examine thoroughly that fellow seeking your hand in marriage. Some are wolves in sheep's clothing, ready to maneuver their way into other people's life to destroy their God-given destiny.

A True Life Story

A sister, a child of God, and a choir member met her future husband in the church–the choir department.

Unknown to the innocent sister, the so-called brother she is courting belongs to the other religion but only joined the church to deceive and marry a decent Christian sister. Most people, including the sister, were impressed by this 'brother' attitude that they never knew his real identity and that he had a covert plan in his heart.

It's not so shocking because the Bible says that the heart of man (or woman) is desperately wicked (Jer. 17:9)

Before long, they got married. The sister gave birth to three children, one after the other. It was after the 3rd child that the "brother" revealed his true identity. He pointedly told the sister his religion and what he worshipped. He warned the sister never to go to the church again.

The sister's joy turned to sadness. What will she do after three children? How will she plot her path? I leave you to proffer answers to those questions. What would have led to this? She might have been carried away by other things or did not pray enough.

Clearly, the so-called brother had a faulty foundation. When the sister got married to him, her entire dreams of a blissful married life collapsed right before her eyes. I pray that will not be your lot in Jesus name.

Just like you cannot compare a house built with cement and concrete to that of mud, you can also not compare marriage built on the Word of God to the Word of men, society, fashion, tradition, or sex.

My dear sisters and brothers, check prayerfully with patience the kind of foundation the potential mate you plan to spend the rest of your life with has.

A lot depends on this. Remember that marriage can make or may your future and that "as you lay on your bed, so you will lie on it." So, one of the building materials that God approves in building a solid and long-lasting marriage is found in His Word:

"But the fruit of the Spirit is Love, Joy, Peace, Longsuffering, Kindness, Goodness, Faithfulness, Gentleness, Self-control. Against such, there is no law." - Gal 5:22-23 (NKJV)

In summary, those nine fruits of the Holy Spirit are the character you and your choice of a marriage partner must possess if you want a solid happy, and long-lasting marital success. I sincerely pray that the Lord Jesus Christ will guide you by His Spirit as long as you permit Him.

Nevertheless, you have an important choice to make. What choice? The next chapter addresses that!

CHOICE

"Choices made wrongly are disastrous. Correct choices you make lead you to profit."

Do not leave your choice of a marriage partner to your parent, relations, friends, or anyone. Why? You will be the one to live with your choice forever!

What Is Choice?

It means selecting or deciding on a particular thing, situation or direction from various varieties. That means you select from two or three options placed before you. It could be a job, where to live, or friends.

Speaking about choice, we are restricting ourselves to the choice of a marriage partner. The choice of marriage partner you make today will speak for your marriage tomorrow.

The choice of marriage partner you make today will paint the picture of the type of marriage you will have tomorrow. The choice you make will determine where you arrive tomorrow, whether into marital bitterness or bliss. Yes, your choice will determine that.

The Bible says concerning choice:

"But if you don't want to worship the LORD then choose here and now… - Joshua 24:15 (CEV)

The above scripture implies that we are created with the right to make our choice. That is why you choose the school you attend, the dress to wear, what to eat, and of course, the God to worship.

Choices are compelling and should not be rushed because you will live with whatever choice you make for the rest of your life, good or otherwise.

An excellent example of a godly choice is found in the story of Ruth, a Moabite. She made the right choice to team up with her mother-in-law, Naomi, and the God of Israel (Ruth 1:10-18). The result? A place in the genealogy of our Lord Jesus Christ (Matt 1:5).

As you plan to marry in the future or maybe a couple of months from now, please carefully and prayerfully examine your prospective mate.

The World is fed up with broken marriages. Divorce has become the norm now in our society. I pray your choice will not result in broken marriage or divorce.

It's also heartwarming to know that God is outrightly against divorce. Hence, you must thoroughly think things through before saying: "I do!"

Like Ruth, team up with God Almighty for wisdom to make the right choice. God says in His Word:

"If any of you lacks wisdom, let him ask of God, who gives to all liberally and without reproach, and it will be given to Him." - James 1:5 (NKJV)

The contemporary English Version renders the above scripture this way:

"If any of you need wisdom, you should ask God, and it will be given to you. God is generous…"

The above scripture is good news to every child of God, including you! Just because you are a graduate does not make you wise to handle the complexities of life.

Oh! You are a master degree holder, great! You have a good and well-paying job with lots of perks, congratulations! Many possess more than these. Sadly, their lives are in shambles. Dear brother and sister, you seriously need the wisdom that God gives to make the right choice.

Another key to making the right choice of a marriage partner is found in the Word of God, and it says:

"With all your heart you must trust the LORD and not your own judgments. Always let Him lead you, and He will clear the road for you to follow. Don't ever think you are wise enough but respect the LORD…" - Prov3:5-7(CEV)

Keep that in mind!

THE VIRTUE OF READING

"During the first year of his reign, I, Daniel, learned from reading the Word of the LORD, as revealed to Jeremiah the prophet, that Jerusalem must lie desolate for seventy years." (Daniel 9:2 NLT)

Reading relevant books on any life's endeavor is important for knowledge. It amazes me to see some intending couples with little or no understanding of marriage. Many enter marriage with a single-mind mentality. Some singles have not read any book on marriage. I don't know how such singles think knowledge and understanding would come.

Getting acquainted with relevant marriage books would put you miles ahead of your peers. With such exposure, your actions and decisions would come from an informed mind. From this moment I would advise you to read a book on marriage every month or every two months.

What Does Reading Give You?

One thing about good books is this: the reader's mind sends a signal of calmness to their whole personality. Reading expands creativity and the ability to make informed decisions. It comes with it the ability to face the future with a clear mind and certainty. Reading makes you a better conversationalist. Books have stopped "bullets" of ignorance. Yes, reading can save your life from bullets of ignorance. Most importantly, you become what you read and listen to repeatedly.

Why Read Books on Marriage?

Before listing why you should read books on marriage, it is instructive for us to consider the Word of God and take some learning.

Matthew 19:3-4 says, "The Pharisees also came unto him, tempting him, and saying unto him, "Is it lawful for a man to put away his wife for every cause?" And he answered and said unto them, "Have ye not read that he which make them at the beginning made them male and female?" KJV (emphasis mine)

We won't delve into the issues relating to divorce in that reference. We are especially keen on the Lord Jesus' response to the questions asked by the Pharisees in bold. "Have you not read," was the response the Pharisees got from Jesus. The Lord Jesus Christ expected they should have read about the issues they brought to Him. He was surprised at their level of ignorance.

When it comes to success in marriage, Christ recommended READING as a prerequisite. Similarly, for singles to make the right choice of a marriage partner, reading relevant marriage books is paramount! Lets now consider why singles ought to read relevant books on marriage:

1. Marriage is a journey every single has never embarked on before. So, they need to partner with people (through their books or messages) who have passed through that route of deciding whom to marry.

2. What you don't know, you will suffer for. Going into a marriage without the correct information will confuse you and eventually consume you. Many go into marriage without knowing what it entails. Their submission is: "My mates are getting married; I should too." What a tragedy! Some are going into marriage because of parents, guardians, and societal pressure. Some are getting married because they have graduated from the university.

3. When you read materials or books on marriage, you will find out what marriage is. Genesis 2:18 talks about the purpose of marriage: "And the

LORD GOD said, 'It is not good for the man to be alone, I will make a helper suitable for him.'" (Emphasis mine).

By reading, prospective couples will know first-hand God's original intention regarding marriage: Companionship or meeting needs. Lack of understanding of this truth is what has turned many marriages into "civil war" of a sort.

From Genesis 2:18, we see that marriage is all about meeting needs. It's not about taking advantage of one another. It is not about oppressing one another. God says concerning man, "I will make a HELPMATE" to meet his need. And this is because there are needs in a man's life that he cannot meet by himself. Also, there are needs in a woman's life that she cannot meet alone.

So God created marriage as a platform for the man to meet the woman's needs and vice versa. This information can only be accessed when singles take it as a project to read relevant books.

And lastly, relevant marriage books help unveil the gender differences between males and females. The reason men behave in a way different from women. Such understanding helps the couple dwell together in unity.

PROPER PRE-MARITAL COUNSELING

The place of proper pre-marital counseling when it comes to marriage cannot be over-emphasized. The Bible declares the importance of counseling by mentorship as what will guarantee safety.

"For by wise counsel thou shall make thy war; and in the multitude of counsellors there is safety." (Proverbs 24:6 KJV)

Making the right choice of a marriage partner is crucial and can be likened to war. Life in itself is war: Warfare and not a fanfare.

The proper counsel from a mentor will give that mentee an edge over mistakes or errors. The proper counsel will provide the recipient with adequate information in choosing the right marriage partner.

The proper counsel is always based upon the infallible Word of God and, if properly understood and adhered to, will yield success. Also, it will bestow upon that individual the grace to make the right choice of marriage partner.

When surrounded by God-fearing counselors/mentors, that individual victory over any form of confusion concerning whom to choose as a marriage partner is guaranteed!

BUILD YOUR RELATIONSHIP ON THE PLATFORM OF LOVE

"For anyone who does not love does not know God-for God is love." - 1Jn 4:8 (NLT)

Someone rightly said that the picture of your future is in the scripture concerning what the Lord Jesus said in John 5:39.

In considering the definition of love, we must dig deep into the scripture. We do not count on the words of psychologists or Romance columnists in Newspapers or magazines. Most of them do not even know God; need we talk more about them serving Him. What then is love according to God's Word?

"Love is patient and kind. Love is not jealous or boastful or proud, or rude. Love does not demand its own way. Love is not irritable, and it keeps no record of when it has been wronged. It is never glad about injustice but rejoices whenever the truth wins out. Love never gives up, never loses faith, is always hopeful, and endures through every circumstance. Love will last forever…" - 1Cor. 13:4-8 (NLT)

You may wonder if the modern-day Christian single sister or brother can possess all the above qualities of love. It is also true that only God is perfect, but God wants all His children to be perfect. (Matt 5:48).

Even if your mate does not possess all these characteristics, they must at least have some with an inclination and readiness to develop. If you are both sure of yourselves and are convinced that God has led you to them, but you notice some awful traits in their life, I'd advise that you both talk it out, seek counsel from mature married Christians and finally take it to God in prayers. The result will thrill and encourage you more. However, everything must be done in sincerity and in fear of God.

Before marriage, I had some issues (weaknesses) to deal with in my life, and the same goes for my wife-to-be. We prayerfully discussed it, and God took control and transformed our lives for the better.

Whenever we are confronted with a situation that can cause us to worry, we will discuss it openly with no pretense and, more often than not, pray about it together. By His grace, our lives and marriage are waxing stronger daily like the Bible says, "The path of the just shinneth more and more unto the perfect day."

Also, God is fulfilling our love life as we allow Him, and our love is growing stronger because His Word also says, "as your days so shall your strength be."

To God be the glory!

LOVE OR LUST

Lust is destructive, but love is constructive; the choice is yours!

Take a closer look at the two words for a moment: Love and Lust.

You will notice that both start with the letter 'L,' but the two words differ significantly in meaning and expression. One is positive and creative. The other is negative and destructive. The former is called love, while the latter is referred to as lust.

Love is of God and originates from Him. He is the source and fountain of love. The Bible says, "for God so loved the World…" (John 3:16) or another expression like "God is love." (1 John 4:8a). Thus, you must have God (Jesus Christ) in your life for you to possess and be a channel of love.

On the other hand, Satan is the source of lust. He is the source and fountain of lust. Satan is destructive as well as passion is. The Bible corroborates this:

"The thief comes only to rob, kill and destroy." - John 10:10a (CEV)

The thief refers to Satan or lust, and its destructive tendencies result in robbing, killing, and destroying people's destinies. Simply put, the attributes of lust are robbing, killing, and destruction. That is why there are many cases of abortion today.

Any fellow (Man/woman) that possesses lust will rob the other of joy, kill their essence, and ultimately destroy their future.

Before you begin to wonder, "where does this leads to?" Let me give you a true-life story (a confession instead) of a lady in a popular Nigerian Newspaper I read some time ago.

The said lady confessed that she has a big problem in her life, despite being a graduate and working in a reputable organization as a manager.

With such a good position and fantastic pay package, what could be her problem, you may ask. She is between 30 to 35 years of age. She confessed to having slept with at least one thousand (1000) men up to date because she craved sex via lust.

Her problem started at the tender age of 17 when she was disvirgined all in the name of love (sorry, lust) between her and her boyfriend. She has not been able to manage any long-term relationships. Only deliverance can set her free from the destructive tendencies of lust.

Listen, dear brother or sister, if your choice of partner encourages sex before marriage, what you two are doing is that you are welcoming and nurturing lust in your life, a destructive foundation for your life.

If a brother or sister tells you it is either sex or no marriage and does not want to reason with the Word of God, walk out of the courtship and thank the Lord for exposing the wrong Choice.

What is happening in this so-called "jet age" as regards promiscuity is alarming. A lot of single guys and girls (including those that are true Christians) see sex as an expression of love. But that is from the pit of hell!

Purpose of Sex

Sex is designed only for the marriage institution for procreation, mutual enjoyment, and release of emotional tension; anything short of this is flagrant abuse with dire consequences.

Why do we have a lot of unwanted pregnancies? What about abortion? It all started with lust (not love). The moment a single lady gets pregnant, the man's so-called love turns to hatred and denial.

For further consequences of lust, please read and meditate on 2 Sam 13: 1-end.

The only place a single Christian brother or sister can find love is among the children of God, those that are believers in the Lord Jesus Christ. So, do not for whatever reason marry an unbeliever. The good Lord will help you to make the right choice.

Further Reading and Mediation:

Consequences of lust 2 Sam 13:1-end

Attributes of love that your choice of a marriage partner should possess. Read: 1Cor. 13:4-8; Gal 5:22-23 (NKJV or NLT or CEV version).

TRUST

"…love always trust…" 1Cor.13:4-8(Easy-to-read version)

"You can't build a life of success on a foundation of lying."

Rev.Richard C Whitcomb

The dictionary defines Trust as a firm belief in the reliability or truth, or strength of a person. Trust and openness are vital for intending couples. Both parties must not hide anything from the person they plan to marry. This is very important.

Are you a child of God? That's commendable! However, if you have a past, open up about your life, especially your weaknesses, during courtship. When this is done, you can both fast and pray about it.

If you have secrets you feel may hunt you and your marriage tomorrow, please let your partner know about them. I don't think keeping secrets from the one you plan to live with for the rest of your life is ideal. You must have confidence in the one you plan to marry; otherwise, there is no point in deceiving yourself.

You must be able to rely on the character of the one you are courting, no matter what anyone says. Trust is therefore very vital in the course of courtship.

Learn to trust one another!

ABSTINENCE FROM SEX

What does the Word abstinence mean?

It means to refrain, to decide not to do something, or to stay away for a particular period, always with a reason for doing so.

What Is Sex?

Pastor Pitan Adeboye of the Redeemed Christian Church of God, in his book, "To Have And To Hold Forever," described or defined sex in the following words:

"Sex is a marital act by which a couple demonstrates their love to each other. It generates pleasure and mutual satisfaction. It is an obligatory act in marriage which is essential for the health of body and soul."

In the past, the issue or things related to sex were not freely discussed. You hardly hear people openly talk about sex. But today, with the wave of the so-called civilization and the exposure of young people to internet pornographic sites and sexually explicit films on cable TV, sex is more freely discussed. Still, we need to know what God says concerning it. The Word of God has answers to every issue of life. Why? Because the Word of God created the World, including the proper use of sex.

Let's search the scripture together:

"Now I will answer the questions that you asked in your letter. You asked," is it best for people not to marry?" 1Cor. 7:1 (CEV)

"But because there is so much sexual immorality, each man should have his own wife, and each woman should have her own husband. The husband should not deprive his wife of sexual intimacy, which is her right as a married woman, nor should the wife deprive her husband." 1Cor. 7:2-3 (NLT)

"A wife belongs to her husband instead of to herself, and a husband belongs to

his wife instead of to himself.

So don't refuse sex to each other unless you agree not to have sex for a little while, in order to spend time in prayer. Then Satan won't be able to tempt you because of your lack of self-control." - 1Cor. 7:4-5 (CEV)

The above scriptural references are pretty long, but it is necessary to have a good view and understanding of what sex is meant for and who is allowed to practice such. The above text summarizes that sexual intimacy, as God permitted, is intended for married couples - couples that are married properly.

Many ladies are living with men with the promise that they will eventually marry and continue to have sex. This is against the Word of God. You don't assume or presume you both are married when the necessary steps have not been taken regarding the marriage ceremony.

The truth is bitter, but it must be told! If you want peace for your life regarding marriage, you had better heed the Word of God. If you are a sister and the brother asking your hand in marriage does not see anything wrong with pre-marital sex, you had better run away from him before he destroys your life.

The reason why there are many failed marriages today can be linked to pre-marital sex.

Couples, even Christians, have extramarital affairs because of the uninhibited sexual practices they had engaged in before marriage.

Sex is like a fruit. If it is not ripe, it leaves a sour-bitter taste on the tongue, but if it is ripe, it leaves a sweet taste.

Reasons why you must not engage in pre-marital sex (i.e., sex before marriage):

- It is a sin against God because you use it for the wrong purpose.
- It can lead to unwanted pregnancy.
- It can lead to hatred from the one professing "love" to you. (Read 2 Sam 13:-end; the story of Amnon and Tamar).
- It can destroy the plan and purpose of God for your life.
- If you are a student, it can cut short your educational aspirations.
- So many ladies, even sisters, have died while carrying out an abortion.
- It can give you a disease you will nurse till you die –AIDS.

If you have been engaging in pre-marital sex and are ready to abstain and save yourself from future marital agony and misery, then go back to the Lord Jesus Christ and ask Him to help you. Go to God in prayers, confess, repent and forsake your sexual sins, for His Words says:

"If we say that we have not sinned, we are fooling ourselves, and the truth is not in our hearts; but if we confess our sins to God, He can always be trusted to forgive us and take our sins away." - 1Jn. 8:9 (CEV)

So, ALL HOPE IS NOT LOST!

PARENTS/GUARDIAN ANGEL

"That's why a man will leave his own father and mother. He marries a woman, and the two of them become like one person." Genesis 2:24 (CEV)

While I will not advise you to disregard your parents/guardian's opinion as to the person you should marry, I must state here that as a child of God, if their opinion or choice negates the Word of God, make them understand why you would not accept their opinion. Before approaching them, pray intensely about it! Why?

You are the one to live with the fellow you plan to marry; hence you must guard against any plan for your parents/guardians to force or pressure you.

For instance, I cannot imagine that a genuine child of God would accept to marry an unbeliever because their parents say so. When problems arise, they may not even be alive to help you. And even if they are alive, they will have little or nothing to do about it. After all, they won't be living with both of you.

Please learn from this story that I am about to share. It may help you or someone you know.

Let's begin!

A True Life Story

I once pastored a church before being transferred to another one. I met a problem that has defied several attempted solutions for years. What was the problem?

There was this sister in the choir department. She is charming and gifted with prophecy, but her marital life was already in shambles and about to collapse. Let's call her sister A. Her husband attempted to strangle her to death or disfigure her whenever he got angry, or there was a little quarrel.

The marriage is already blessed with two beautiful children: a girl and a boy. It was discovered later that the husband, who is supposed to be a child of God, smokes cigarettes, even marijuana. Can you imagine that?

Sister A recalled a day the man beat the living daylights out of her. She said she almost died if not for the intervention of her neighbors.

While counseling, I asked her if she knew the man as a child of God before agreeing to marry him. Sister A answered that her late mother made her marry the man, thinking he was a genuine Christian.

Her answer was YES when I asked her if she prayed about it. God showed her a revelation that meant she shouldn't marry the man, but I think because of pressure, she dis-regarded this revelation from God.

The Bible says, "There is a way that seems right to a man, but its end is the way of death." Prov. 14:12 (NKJV).

Sister A's late mother's decision, as she made us understand, led to her marrying the wrong person – a way that seems right but ends up in the death of her marriage.

Sadly, the marriage collapsed after two children and several beatings and marks on the sister.

Please, I am not saying you should not carry your parent/guardians along; they have a role to play. If they fail to see reason with you as regards God's will, please fast and pray about it with your partner while carrying your pastor along. NEVER MARRY WITHOUT YOUR PARENT'S APPROVAL. TO DO OTHERWISE IS DANGEROUS!

My sincere prayer is that you will not make the wrong choice!

GOD'S LEADING

"The Lord always help those who are determined to do His will." Pastor E.A Adeboye.

God is a good God. He has a unique plan for all his children, including you. How do I know this? His Word says so:

"For I know the plans I have for you," says the LORD." They are plans for good and not for disasters to give you a future and a hope." - Jer. 29:11 (NLT)

From the above scripture, you will be convinced that God has a plan for you and, by extension, your marital future.

"I will bless you with a future filled with hope - a future of success, not of suffering."

Once again, dear reader, God is interested in the success of your marriage. He does not want you to endure your marriage. That is why you must ask him to lead you regarding whom to choose as your marriage partner. Not just any self-acclaimed born-again sister or brother, but the one with whom two of you will fulfill God's purpose for your lives here on earth.

You are born with an assignment, a destiny. To fulfill that destiny on the marriage platform, you must not make any mistake with the choice of marriage partner.

God is saying:

"Come now, let's settle this…" - Is. 1:18 (NLT)

God is pleading:

"I, the LORD, invite you to come and take it over…" Is. 1:18 (CEV)

God is saying:

"… Come, let's discuss these things…" - Is.1:18 (Easy to read)

If you meditate on His Words and pray, your marital future can be a success. You need to discuss your choice with the Lord based upon His Words for you to have a good foundation and marital success.

For instance, considering an unbeliever for a marriage partner is entirely out of the blue print of the Word of God. For you to make your choice of marriage partner outside His Word is a recipe for disaster!

Bishop David Oyedepo says, "no matter the counsel, dream, or vision, there is no meeting point between a Christian and a sinner. The Abrahamic covenant demands that you marry among your kinsmen only. You are not permitted to marry strangers."

Listen! No matter how you feel about it or how much you would have loved to, an unbeliever is out of the question for a believer.

Here is what God says about it:

"You are not the same as those people who don't believe. So don't join yourselves to them. Good and bad don't belong together. Light and darkness cannot fellowship (sharing). How can Christ and Belial (The devil) have any agreement? What can a believer have together with a non-believer? God's temple cannot have any agreement with idols. And we are the temple of the living God. Like God said. 'I will live with them and walk with them, I will be their God, and they will be my people." - 2 Cor. 6:14-16 (Easy to read)

Dear Brethren, when you are determined to do His will, no matter the obstacles or challenges, God will help you! He will create a way of escape for you, only be determined to do His will not only for marriage but in every area of your life.

CHRISTIAN COURTSHIP

"Two people will not walk together unless they agree." - Amos 3:3 (Easy to read)

"Can two people walk together without agreeing on the direction?" - Amos 3:3 (NLT)

What is Christian Courtship?

Christian Courtship is a period before wedding/marriage where a Christian brother and sister agree about so many issues and see if they both share the same vision, hope, and aspiration about marriage. "Courtship is an adopted word to describe the Biblical model for the relationship between a man and a woman that leads to marriage."

From the Word of God quoted above, we can reliably infer that Christian courtship involves two people who have agreed to walk together in the direction of marriage (not sleeping together before marriage).

Dearly beloved brother or sister, marriage is spiritual and orderly. It must be treated with the utmost respect. Thus, the Christian Courtship is very important for intending brother and sister that have agreed to marry.

During the Courtship, a proper biblical foundation must be laid down to have a happy married life.

Despite the enormous responsibilities and challenges that come with marriage, yours can bear that totem "happy married life" that God plans for you as His child. The Bible says he has made us both Priest and kings (and queens). - (Rev.1:6). So for a Christian brother, he is a king while the sister is a queen (Please smile at that).

A king must have a queen to establish a royal family, which God also intended for His children as established in 1Pet. 2:9. God wants your marriage to be a kind of "Heaven on Earth."

Hence, before you venture into wedding plans, you must agree on many things like what you both want for your marriage. Both of you must realize that marriage means TILL DEATH DO US PART!

The word "agree" from Amos 3:3 is profound. You need to ask yourself, "Do we agree." "Are we walking towards a common goal?"

You don't need to fast and pray before you answer those questions.

If your choice of a marriage partner is worried about your involvement in church activities, then there is a problem. If they are uncomfortable with your reading the Bible or speaking in tongue, then I don't think you are heading in the same direction. If they are someone that finds it challenging to give and pay tithe regularly, then you shouldn't bother them.

Agreement on what direction you want your marriage to go can only be attained on the platform of courtship. The following are excerpts (as regards courtship) from the book by one of my spiritual fathers: Bishop David Oyedepo, titled "Bible sense for getting into marriage."

After proposing to a lady and she agrees to marry you, the next thing to do is obey the Biblical injunction to prove all things. (1Thes 5:21)

The courtship period is the time to prove your relationship. Yes, your spirit agrees that you have made the right choice, but you still need to verify everything.

Courtship is a fact-finding period. Marriage without courtship naturally ends in crisis because there was no opportunity to get to know each other and prove whether the choice made was wise or not.

Impatience is responsible for many marriage failures in the western world today.

Courtship can be broken. This should not be mistaken for divorce. If your ideas and ideals are not similar, common-sense demands that you quit.

(Author's note; don't make it a habit of breaking your courtship at the slightest excuse)

Courtship is a covenant culture for a successful marriage. One month is not sufficient. Two months is risky. Man is a complex being.

The proving process is the personal responsibility of the individuals involved because they are the ones to live together. Do not allow your parents or family to prove your spouse for you.

My final note on courtship is that secretly indulging in bodily, emotional, and sexual pleasure at this stage with your marriage partner is a sin. It is a potential sign of marital failure.

NO ROOM FOR DIVORCE

"The Lord God of Israel says, "I hate divorce. And I hate the cruel things that men do so protect your spiritual unity. Don't cheat on your wife." - Mal. 2:16 (Easy to read)

Divorce means to set free, undo a bond, give liberty, to release or cut apart. A legal divorce is the absolute end of a marriage contract while two parties are still alive.

In the Bible, Moses initiated or permitted it. (read Deut 24:1-4). However, the Lord Jesus disannulled it, thus restoring the original status of marriage. "In the beginning, it was not so." (Matt 19:4-8).

The summary of the whole thing is that God hates divorce.

Dear sister or brother, if God hates divorce, you have a responsibility to think deeply and pray with understanding before you go into marriage because once you marry, there is no room for divorce.

The Bible describes divorce as a 'cruel thing,' and I can tell you that society suffers from this.

The short and long-term negative impact divorce has on individuals, children, the extended family, the church, and society is enormous.

Hence before you agree on marriage with your partner, please carry God along. God is the Architect of marriage; He designed it for companionship, fellowship, procreation, sexual enjoyment, and so on. He made it to be a permanent union, "TILL DEATH DO US PART."

God has a tremendous and positive plan for the marriage institution, but Satan has come to steal, kill and destroy (Jn. 10:10a).

However, the good news for marriage is revealed by the Rock of Ages, and it's found in the infallible Biblical principles at 1Jn. 5:4, 5.

"For whatsoever is born of God overcomes the world. And this is the victory that has overcome the world - our faith.

Who is he who overcomes the world, but he who believes that Jesus is the Son of God? - 1Jn 5:4, 5 (NKJV)

Listen, my dear brother or sister: MARRIAGE HAS ITS PECULIAR CHALLENGES. IT HAS ITS UPS AND DOWNS.

Unfortunately, would-be couples prepare for the wedding of just one day and neglect the marriage that will last for the rest of their lives.

To overcome the plans of Satan and divorce, make sure the brother or sister you intend to marry is born of God and believes in the Lord Jesus Christ, i.e., DON'T EVER MARRY AN UNBELIEVER NO MATTER WHAT, ELSE YOU WILL PAY FOR IT!

It is a matter of life and death. There are a lot of sad stories, agony, and sorrow that result from marrying an unbeliever.

May the Lord help your decisions in Jesus name.

JOURNEY TO MARRIAGE (THE PREPARATION)

"The preparations of the heart in man, and the answer of the tongue, is from God." - (Proverbs 16:1 KJV emphasis mine)

Someone rightly said, "Success is where preparation and opportunity meet." Choosing the right marriage partner is not a guessing game but a deliberate preparation with adequate, relevant marriage information.

Preparation in whatever an individual embarks on is very crucial. Shoddy preparation leads to frustration and failure. Deliberate and well-planned preparation lead to peace of mind and fulfillment.

However, God has a role to play in an individual preparation, and if peradventure God is excluded, that project would fail. Many have excluded God and His Word when choosing a marriage partner, and afterward, one sad story or the other. The Bible says that unless God builds a house, those involved in the building do it in vain. (Psalm 127:1)

On the other hand, if God is honoured and made part of the plans from the onset of that project, the end product will be fulfillment and success. (Joshua 1:8) The Bible says, when we acknowledge God in all our ways of preparation, He will automatically direct our planning and ensure it succeeds.

About Man's Role?

Listen to this: What God can do, man cannot, and what man will do, God would not. Therefore, man has a role to play in choosing whom to marry.

Looking at Proverbs 16:1, apart from the key points—God and man— other vital points stood out — the heart and the tongue!

A man should first and foremost prepare the heart by feeding it with the correct information. Through the Holy Spirit, God will search out from the minds and see if the relevant information in the recesses of the heart is in line with the project. Once the Holy Spirit validates, He directs speech, responds to situations as they come, and ensures the individual makes the right choice of marriage partner.

Marriage preparation involves getting the proper knowledge and understanding of what marriage is all about. Marriage preparation entails that we prepare our heart correctly by feeding it with the correct relevant information that would aid our decision-making before and after marriage.

Preparing our minds for marriage comes via reading the right books, listening to the right audio messages, and attending relevant marriage seminars. In choosing the right marriage partner, that individual heart must first be corrected.

The Bible says that the heart is deceitful and beyond cure. Who can understand it? (Jeremiah 17:9 NIV).

That is why God recommended re-formatting our hearts after giving our lives to the Lord Jesus Christ. The heart has to be cultivated with the Word of God. Otherwise, our decision-making process would be flawed and lead to unpleasant situations.

Why Must the Heart be Prepared?

A defective heart produces defective decision-making processes.

The heart of an unregenerate man is desperately selfish, wicked, and incapable of making godly decisions.

The future is created from the heart factory. So if the heart is crooked, the future will be full of regrets and sorrow.

Therefore, Christian singles must ensure regular reading of the Word of God. This brings about growth and ensures the heart is aligned with the thought of God. By so doing, decision-making in the way that pleases God will become very easy.

Further Bible references to ponder over: 1 Peter 2:2; Romans 12:1-2.

PRAYERS

Pray so that you do not become prey.

I believe so much in the power of prayers as a Christian. It has a tremendous force in bringing to reality your heart-felt desires or goals in every endeavour of life, including your choice of a marriage partner.

What Is Prayer?

It is a solemn request or thanksgiving to God Almighty. The Bible says: "Unless the LORD builds the house they labour in vain who build it unless the LORD guards the city. The watchman stays awake in vain." - Psalm. 127:1 (NKJV)

Dear friends, you will agree that the above scriptures do not need any explanation. They are very lucid and simple to understand to a discerning mind. Many people have made mistakes about their choice of marriage partner because they never really bothered about praying.

Prayer changes situations! It makes impossibility possible.

For instance, if both intending couples are so sure of God's leading but your parents and guardians don't support you based on tribe or cultural difference, go to God in prayers.

God says. "Call upon me in the day of trouble, and I will answer you." - Jer. 33:3

Also, God says that the king's heart is in His hands (Prov. 21:1).

I remember that when the list of traditional items for my engagement was sent to me, I was prepared not to buy some items on the list. These are cartons of Guilder & Stout. This is because God hates alcohol. It was a big challenge to our wedding, but my wife and I agreed, based on the Word of God, that we weren't going to buy alcohol. We prayed, and God answered us.

God made them (our parents) forget about the alcoholic items during the engagement. Glory be to God in the Highest! Remember, the Bible says, "for with God nothing shall be impossible." - (Luke 1:37).

FINAL THOUGHTS

Please feel free to write me at courtshipguide@gmail.com for your testimonies or comments. As you put these guides into practice, I see God helping you choose the marriage partner according to His purpose and plan for you.

If you have read this book and have not given your life to the Lord Jesus Christ before, here is an opportunity for you. Unless you invite Him into your life, you can NEVER fulfill the purpose of God for your life.

Please pray thus:

"O Lord God, I come to you in the Name of Jesus Christ. Your Word says, '...whosoever shall call on the name of the Lord shall be saved.'(Acts 2:21).

Please, Lord Jesus, come into my life; I accept You as my Lord and Personal Saviour. I receive eternal life into my spirit and according to Your Word in Romans 10:9, which says: 'That if thou shalt confess with thy mouth the Lord Jesus and shall believe in thine heart that God hath raised Him from the dead, thou shall be saved.'"

I declare that I am saved; I am born-again; I am a child of God! From today, I walk in the consciousness of my new life in Christ Jesus. Amen

Congratulations, you are now a child of God! Please asks the Lord in prayers to lead you to a Bible-believing church. The Redeemed Christian Church of God is one such church by His grace. Feel free to join any of our parishes in your locality.

God bless you!

PRAYING FOR A LIFE PARTNER

The Bible says that we ought to pray always and not give up. - See Luke 18:1. It also adds that the effectual fervent prayers of a righteous individual or group bring forth results. - See James 5:17.

Based on the above Bible references, we are confident that when we pray according to His Will, God hears and answers. - See 1John5:14.

Find below sample prayers for praying for a life partner, and as you pray out of a pure heart, God will answer speedily in Jesus name.

Father, deal with every form of an idol in my heart in Jesus 'name – Judges 14:1-3

I decree that the Lord will provide for me the bones of my bones and the flesh of my flesh – Genesis 2:23

I refuse to marry wrongly in the name of Jesus.

Father, give me the grace to be able to discover your perfect will for my life – Romans 12:1-2

I declare myself free from every unprogressive relationship in the name of Jesus.

I declare myself free from every ungodly attachment in the name of Jesus. – 2 Corinthians 6:14-18

Father, let your counsel only stand in my marital life – Psalms 33:10-11

I reject every proposal designed to rub me off the glory of God.

Father, I hold on to your promises, let my day of joy come quickly – Psalms 30:5; Isaiah 40:30-31

I decree that my marriage will be a model to the glory of God.

Father, grant me good speed and let everything work together for my good. – Genesis 24:12; Romans 8:28

Father, I oppose every Laban that says I will not be able to prepare and plan for my own home in Jesus' name.- Genesis 30:25-27

Also, by the grace of God, there is a blog dedicated to the course of Christian Singles with insightful and value-adding articles for your reading pleasure and spiritual education. The blog's theme is: "COURTSHIP GUIDE FOR CHRISTIAN SINGLES IN PREPARATION FOR MARRIAGE."

The following topics are available for reading pleasure and spiritual education:

The consequences of sexual sins series

How do sexual sins relate to soul tie

The gift of singleness

Courtship guide series. How to guard your heart.

Don't go into marriage with a single person's mindset...

Thank you for purchasing this eBook. It shows that you are concerned about your marital future. I assure you that if you diligently and prayerfully apply the principles in this book, you will never be confused in Jesus' name.

Congratulations, and I pray from my heart that God perfect all that concerns you in Jesus' name.

www.ingramcontent.com/pod-product-compliance
Lightning Source LLC
LaVergne TN
LVHW052052160826
845678LV00015B/3181

* 9 7 9 8 8 4 4 4 5 4 7 0 7 *